Cyberbullying:

Bystanders and Victims

JOSH GUNDERSON

JOSH GUNDERSON

CYBERBULLYING

ISBN-13: 978-1545274064

CONTENTS

1	Introduction	1
2	Understanding Bullying	3
3	Why Is Cyberbullying Different?	7
4	How Is Cyberbullying Accomplished?	11
5	Warning Signs of Bullying	15
6	The Victims	17
7	The Bystanders	21
8	The Bullies	25
9	Student Response to Bullying	29
10	Parent Response to Bullying	33
11	Educating the Bullies	39
12	What Our Schools Can Do	41
13	Wrap Up	43
14	About the Author	45

JOSH GUNDERSON

Introduction

Greetings and welcome to **Cyberbullying: Perpetrators, Bystanders and Victims**. Back in 2012 I was asked to create a program designed to address the topic of bullying, specifically surrounding the topic of cyberbullying. The workshop that came from this has quickly become one of my most popular.

The problem, I have found, with workshops is the time constraints that typically come from them within conference or community settings. We never seem to have enough time to cover everything. Many times I have had to cut out question and answer time to be able to get to each subject I've wanted to cover.

In an effort to curb this problem I have sat down and written this book. What follows is designed to work on its own or a supplement to any of my workshops.

Is this a perfect book? As much as I would like to believe so, the answer is no. There is so much to this topic that it is very easy to be bogged down. As I sat down to work on the material for this book, even I was overwhelmed.

Additional information about my programs is

available on my web site at **www.joshgunderson.com** and I am, of course, available by email for any questions. Even more information and updates can be found on my blog.

I thank you for purchasing this book and hope you find the information within to be valuable.

Understanding Bullying

Many times I have been told that bullying is just "kids being kids." This is a mentality that I have encountered on multiple occasions while working all over the country and it can be a dangerous one. While bullying is something that we all may have encountered growing up, the dynamic has changed and evolved over the years as we have become more and more connected through technology, specifically through social media.

Now the bullying many of us faced or witness hasn't gone away but we were only familiar with the three main branches of bullying: physical, verbal and relational.

Physical Bullying

Physical bullying is one of the most prevalent and obvious forms of peer-to-peer harassment. This is when the aggressor uses acts of physical violence against another person. This is what usually what comes to mind when people thing of bullying and historically receives more attention from schools.

These bullies tend to have the advantage of strength over their victim and their attacks involve hitting, punching, shoving and other physical attacks.

Think the old sitcom go-to of shoving someone into a locker or throwing them into a garbage can.

Verbal Bullying

Verbal bullying harnesses the power of name-calling and insults against its victims in an effort to gain power. Perpetrators tend to use this method to constantly harass and belittle their victims with slews of insults typically targeted at physical characteristics, behavior or perceived social standing.

Verbal bullying is typically one of the most difficult to identify as it becomes a situations of one student's word against another as this is typically carried out when adults are not present.

This is also a behavior that is often brushed off and victims are instructed to just simply ignore their aggressor in an effort to make them stop.

Relational Bullying

Relational bullying, also referred to as emotional bullying, relies on social manipulation. This can often include a bullying spreading rumors, ostracizing others, manipulating groups or friends in an effort to sabotage the social standing of one person while raising their own.

Relational bullying is more common in girls

typically within the middle school years but often extends into the upper grades.

Relational bullying is not just limited to schools and is commonplace in cases of workplace bullies or "bully bosses."

Cyberbullying

Cyberbulling is something of a newcomer to the scene with the first prevalent case in 2006 with the suicide of Megan Meier after being harassed through a social networking site. Cyberbullying gained worldwide attention following a string of bullying-related suicides in the fall of 2009, particularly within the LGBTQ+ community.

Cyberbullying relies on technology, namely social media, and a tool in the harassment of another person. This can include text messaging, posting inappropriate or harmful images of another person, or making threats against another.

Cyberbullying does carry similarities to the previously covered types of bullying but does hold some very strong differences which set it apart, these will be discussed in the next chapter.

One of the biggest problems when it comes to cyberbullying revolves around a lack of understanding of the many forms of communication that kids are utilizing today.

JOSH GUNDERSON

Why Is Cyberbullying Different?

When it comes to bullying the ability to conduct this behavior through technology and social media has changed the game. The dangerous mentality of "kids just being kids" can't be applied because the methods and results are far more malicious than they were in the past.

While cyberbullying does share many similar components in terms of traditional bullying, there are some key factors that set it apart.

Round the Clock Access

In our brave new world of social media we are connected in ways that allow us to have almost 24/7 access to one another. This is a major factor in the growth of the cyberbullying trend and has been a game changer when it comes to bullying.

When I look back on being bullied in high school, it was something that happened during school hours and I was able to escape one the day had ended. Now we have almost limitless access to one another and this has allowed the bullies to follow their victims home.

Worldwide Audience

The internet has changed the way we share just about everything and bullying is no exception to this. While traditional bullying occurs in front of a limited audience, bullying online can be viewed by just about anyone that happens to come across the bully's post.

Many times these posts end up going viral before anything is done to stop it. In one case a student was attacked in the hallway by classmates and a video of the incident surfaced online, racking up thousands of views worldwide before it was reported and removed by the host site.

Anonymity

While many social media sites and apps offer fun ways to share and connect with others, there are some that have great intentions with disastrous results. Sites like Ask.FM and YikYak allow users to remain anonymous as they interact with one another. This has lead to instances of cyberbullying as there is no way knowing who is posting or sending messages.

At the same time, many sites do not do anything to verify the identity of their users which allows bullies to create fake profiles. These manufactured identities give bullies a false sense of security to attack victims with little fear of repercussion.

Permanence

One key thing about the internet that people are constantly forgetting is that it is forever. Even when pictures and videos are removed, the chances of them being found elsewhere are high. It doesn't take much to save a file or screenshot an image.

Even if a victim is able to move past the incident, there is a good chance of it coming back around again in the future.

Inescapable

Cyberbullying can be omnipresent. While it's easy to get away from a bully in a face-to-face encounter, with technology the bully can follow their targets just about anywhere. This can leave the victim feeling as if they have no control or escape from their attacker.

JOSH GUNDERSON

How Cyberbullying Is Accomplished

With each form of traditional bullying, the methods are fairly straightforward. With cyberbullying the methods are seemingly endless. With that in mind I have narrowed list down to some of the most common tactics used in cyberbullying cases.

Exclusion

In this vein, cyberbullies are taking a page out of the traditional bully book. In this tactic the bullies will take to excluding their victims from online events. This can include not inviting them to join certain pages or groups on social media, deleting their comments or ignoring them all together. This behavior is often mirrored in the real world as well for the maximum effect.

Harassment

In the context of cyberbullying harassment comes in the form of hurtful messages being sent by text, chat or posts on social media.

Flaming

This term refers to leading a victim into a heated argument within an online forum usually leading to harassment to an extreme level in a very public way.

Outing

This is the act of taking someone's private information (via email or texts) and making them public knowledge. An example of this would be someone revealing a crush on a person in their class to a friend, that friend then forwards the conversation to that crush or other people who were not involved in that private conversation.

This method is often used when it comes to sexually explicit photos or messages that have been shared among peers.

Phishing

One of the tactics used to create a situation for outing is phishing which involves tricking someone into sharing personal information often through lies, deception messages or using a fake profile to befriend someone online.

Happy Slapping

A fad that originated in the United Kingdom, happy slapping involves a person or group of people assaulting a person at random while filming the encounter to post online.

Imping (Impersonation)

One of the most extreme forms of cyberbullying involves the bully creating a online account using their victims name and photo and using this profile to create a poor reputation for their target. Often using foul language, posting embarrassing images or using the account to harass others.

JOSH GUNDERSON

Warning Signs of Bullying

It is here that I am allowing the worlds of bullying to collide in this conversation. This is mostly because when it comes to what parents and educators needs to look out for in cases of cyberbullying, the same applies to all situations of bullying.

It is important to realize that every situation is not the same and that goes for children as well.

For parents, a big part of being able to recognize these signs is being sure to be involved in your child's day-to-day life. Make a point to check in with them regularly about their day. This allows you to be able to recognize when something seems off.

Again, I have narrowed this down to some of the more common warning signs but these may vary depending on the situation or your child.

1. Seems uneasy about going to school.
2. Regularly feigning illness to avoid school or other social settings.
3. Depression or aggression, particularly following computer use.
4. Acts nervous when receiving messages or texts.
5. Trouble sleeping.
6. Unexplained weight gain or loss.

7. Withdrawing from friends and family in the offline world.
8. Insomnia or regular nightmares.
9. A decline in performance in school including a drop in grades or participation.
10. Self destructive behaviors including but not limited to drug and alcohol use or thoughts of suicide.

As a parent or educator, if you begin to spot these signs or event suspect something might be going on, it is important to begin a conversation early. Sometimes knowing that someone is paying attention is enough to lay the groundwork to preventing more serious issues down the line.

The Victims

Anyone who has taken part in any of my workshops knows that I am not big on using statistics in my programs and I am doing my best to avoid them here. The reason for this is how easily these numbers can be manipulated and how quickly they can change.

The fact of the matter is that every year students, number in the thousands, skip school every year as a result of bullying. As the effects of bullying take hold, often times the cause goes untreated simply because kids can be reluctant to step forward and report the issue.

The reasons can vary from person to person but a lot of the time students are just unsure how to handle the situation and resort to keeping quiet while they attempt to work things out for themselves.

It's important to understand reasons why kids may be reluctant to come forward about being the victim of bullying so a proactive approach can be taken.

They Are Afraid Of Retaliation

All too often, victims of bullying feel that reporting the issue will do nothing to help them. The general feeling seems to be that by reporting a bully, it will only escalate the problem once it's found out they've "tattled" and enduring further abuse and labeled a snitch.

Concern That They Won't Be Taken Seriously

It is not uncommon for students to come speak with me following workshops and a comment I receive quite often is that they feel that the grown-ups in their lives won't actually do anything to help them. Sadly, this is true in many cases of reported bullying when student report what is going on and the adult has failed to take action or has ignored them completely. This is where the "kids just being kids" mentality fails victims of bullying and can lead to distrust of adults who are supposed to be there to help.

They Feel Embarrassed/Ashamed

Bullying is very often about power, manipulation and control and the desired effect is the make the victim feel weak. This powerless feeling can lead the victim to feeling ashamed that they are unable to stand up for themselves. Kids, and even adults, often feel embarrassed when they need to ask for help and as a result tend to avoid doing so.

They Fear They Will Get In Trouble

This is especially true in cases of cyberbullying. Most kids won't admit they are being targeted by bullies because they fear that parents or teachers will restrict their access to technology and social media which would only serve to further outcast them from their peers. This fear will cause kids to think twice about reporting bullying instances.

JOSH GUNDERSON

The Bystanders

When it comes to bullying, in many cases there are more than just the bully and the victim involved. So much emphasis is put on these two primary parties that quite often the third party involved in bullying goes unnoticed: the bystander.

Overall bystanders are those who are witness to bullying but are not directly involved. From there bystanders fall into three categories: Hurtful, passive, and helpful.

Hurtful bystanders are those who may instigate the bullying by prodding those involved into a altercation. Others may encourage the bullying behavior by laughing at the victim or cheering at what they are witnessing. Some may join in once the bullying has begun.

Passive bystanders are those who witness the bullying taking place, whether it's online or off, and do nothing. These bystanders unwittingly contribute to the problem by providing the attention and audience a bully often craves and their silence allows bullies to continue their behavior.

Helpful bystanders are those who take action against bullying. This can happen by direct intervention- standing up to the bully, defending the victim or redirecting the situation away from bullying. Another way to be a helpful bystander would be by getting help to stop the bullying either by getting an adult involved or getting other bystanders to stand up against the bully in a non-violent way.

Helpful bystanders can also play an important role when it comes to cyberbullying. Many social media sites and applications have taken steps to ensure a safe experience for their users. This has included reporting tools specifically targeted towards online bullies. Encourage students to take advantage of these. Furthermore, when they encounter a link to a video or photo that is being disseminated, they break that cycle by not forwarding it on to others. When possible they should save posts and share them with a trusted adult.

As a part of bullying prevention education, it's important to make sure a focus is placed on empowering bystanders and letting them know that they have an amazing power in the fight against bullying and it's important that they use their voice.

Many bystanders will not speak out much for the same reasons that victims don't. They can fear retaliation from the bully, fear they won't be taken seriously or may just feel that the situation is none of their business as it doesn't directly affect them.

It is important during the course of education

students on the topic of bullying prevention to really empower each and every one of them to take action. When I am speaking to students in assemblies and workshops this is one of the major points that I make sure to emphasize to them.

I, very often, share real life stories of bullying with students in an effort to make it more real for them. These stories are often tragic and elicit strong emotions from my audiences, regardless of age. It's important to harness this emotion and help turn it into action. It's important to realize that in any instance of bullying there is always someone who has the power to make a difference and possibly save a life.

At some point in time, that person just might be them.

JOSH GUNDERSON

The Bullies

Why do bullies bully? This is a question I get a lot and one that I think is important to ask. We often forget that when it comes to situations of bullying as so much emphasis is placed on treating and caring for the victim. Most times, the bully is simply punished and that's all she wrote.

It is in this that many victims feel like enough wasn't done to protect them in the future. It's important for parents and educators to not only understand the root of the bullying but also work to curb this type of behavior going forward.

Over the past ten years I have heard of many reasons why bullying takes place either at school, online or in the workplace. While the reasons greatly vary and seem endless, they can really be boiled down to the following:

Power

Bullies feel an overwhelming desire to be in control, to have power over any given situation. Often times bullies themselves feel weak and use physical strength over others to feel in control. This can be true among "mean girl" bullies as well as within athletes turned bully. In each, they thrive on having power or control over those they perceive to be either physically or emotionally weaker than them.

Boredom

The sad truth is, especially in cases of cyberbullying, this behavior often stems from boredom. It is during the summer months and vacation time that we tend to see a spike in bullying behavior from teens especially. This behavior provides entertainment and a source of drama to spice things up a little bit. This will also stem from a lack of supervision and they are acting out as a way to gain attention.

Prejudice

One of the most common reasons for bullying stems from the aggressor attacking someone else for being different. Kids may target someone with special needs or allergies or simply single someone out for their race, religion or sexual orientation. When it comes down to it, prejudice is typically at the root of most cases of bullying.

Bandwagon

In some cases of bullying we see others participating because of peer pressure or a desire to fit in with the popular crowd, even if it means going against their better judgment. There is also a fear that if they do not participate they, in turn, will become a target for aggression.

Problems At Home

Children that come from abusive homes are more likely to display aggressive, bullying behavior towards others at school or online. This is also true for kids whose parents are often absent from the home environment. This gives the bully a sense of power and control over their lives by acting out against others. Bullying among siblings can also carry over to bullying in the schoolyard to help the victim regain a feeling of power and control.

Lack of Empathy

Many times, in cases of bullying, the aggressor lacks an ability to recognize the needs or feelings of others. In many cases, they derive pleasure from watching others in pain. This is seen a lot in cases of cyberbullying as the aggressor has no physical connection to their victim. It is a lot easier to hurt someone when you don't have to see the direct result of your actions.

JOSH GUNDERSON

Student Response To Bullying

When working with students my advice when it comes to responding to bullies has remained the same throughout the last ten years. This is the advice that was given to me when I was in high school and dealing with my own bullies. While some of this has had to evolve with the times over the years, the general message remains the same.

Here are the tips that I share with students:

Don't Respond

As we've discussed, bullies are all about power and the gain satisfaction in knowing they have control over someone. When their victim doesn't respond or acknowledge them, they lose some of that power. Sometimes the best way to respond is to just walk away from the situation if at all possible. The same goes for online bullying. More often than not, when people don't engage with the behavior it will resolve itself.

This may not always be the case but this a good first step in dealing with a bully.

Don't Retaliate

This is a hard one and I am very understanding of that fact. When someone attacks us, hurts us we want to fight back. Our every instinct can be to fight back but the truth of the matter is that this only puts the victim in a position to be labeled a bully as well and get themselves in trouble.

Obviously, if someone is in physical danger and backed into a corner, by all means, defend yourself. But in many cases, particularly cyberbullying, and eye for an eye is never the ideal.

Save the Evidence

When it comes to cyberbullying in particular, the upside is that the evidence is right there. Screenshot conversations save text messages and keep a log of what is happening. This was you have what you need to prove there is a situation of bullying.

Block the Bully

One of the many upsides of social media is that if you don't want someone talking to you, you can block them. This is a common feature among many popular social networks and applications and I highly encourage everyone taking advantage of them. There are even features on your phone that can be used to block texts and calls from certain numbers.

Talk to A Trusted Adult

It is important that kids know that they can reach out to someone in a time of need. Whether it is a teacher, administrator, parent or relative, it's important to share with someone what is going on. They can help work through the situation and offer resources.

Be a Friend, Not a Bystander

It's important to realize that when you witness situations of bullying, whether online or off, and you do nothing, say nothing, you are just as guilty as the bully. It's important to be an upstander in these situations and give voice to them. This can be as simple as involving an adult when you see something happing. The important thing is to do something.

Take Time to Think

Any student that has been a part of one of my workshops can tell you that, above all, the biggest thing I will ask of them is to take the time to think, to think about themselves and one another on a human level. To know that, regardless of what we think we know about each other, we are all human beings with thoughts, emotions and dreams. It's important to remember that as we go about our day to day lives, we are all fighting different battles.

Cyberbullies

When it comes to bullies in the online world, it's important that students take steps to protect themselves. Taking a look at privacy settings and friends lists are key to ensuring that bullies are kept out. Everyone wants the highest friend and follower count possible these days but that "internet fame" comes with a heavy price. It's important to keep things like phone number and screen names private. The same goes for passwords. Kids are, all too often, far too comfortable sharing passwords with friends and this is a practice that needs to be ended.

Parent Response to Bullying

Okay. I'm going to get painfully candid here for a moment. Were this one of my workshops, there would be more of a lighthearted atmosphere surrounding our discussions of these topics. Part of the reason I resisted writing something like this for so long is because I felt it would lack my voice. I feel I teach better when the audience is directly in front of me.

I am not a parent. As of sitting down to write this I have no children so I can't even pretend to imagine how difficult it can be for a parent to find out their child has become the victim of bullying. However, I have spent the better part of the last decade working with bullied children and their parents. The advice that I have here stems from these conversations, workshops and exchanges.

My advice also comes from how I was raised and how the adults in my life have responded to instances of bullying.

Like with students, I encourage parents to keep a log of instances of bullying. Realize that bullying is defined as a repeated behavior so having evidence of this is important in the long run.

It is also important to stay knowledgeable about

these issues. Event with a world of knowledge at our fingertips, we sometimes find ourselves in a bubble. Many times when I'm speaking about specific instances of bullying, stories that have made world news, parents have no idea that these occurred.

Once I was speaking in a town where a cyberbullying situation had not only occurred but became a commonly used case study. No one knew what I was talking about when I brought it up.

I encourage parents to keep tabs on current events and share these stories with their kids. It is in this that we can help them find empathy for one another and realize the effect that their words and actions can have on others.

Along that same line, I highly encourage everyone to look into their state's anti-bullying laws. As of today, all fifty states do have some sort of anti-bullying law in place that outlines the responsibilities of both parents and schools. One problem is a lack of consistency in these laws as many still do not define cyberbullying within them.

One of the best resources for learning about your state's law and where it stands compared to others is by visiting bullypolice.org. This organization not only outlines the laws but grades them based on rigorous standards. I encourage all to take a look at these ratings and work alongside their community and lawmakers to strengthen their laws.

If you take a look at some of the grades earned by states, the highest grade (A++) have been rewarded to states who's laws were redrafted following high-profile cases of bullying related suicide. These laws were reactionary.

This is the most dangerous thing we can do, waiting for something to happen before we chose to do anything about it.

From there, as I mentioned previously, it's important that parents maintain an open and constructive line of communication with their children. I'm not saying that it's important to be your child's best friends, but you do want them to feel comfortable coming to you with problems they may be having.

If your child does approach you with an issue like being bullied, the best thing you can do for them is remain calm. They are already in a vulnerable state and your getting overly emotional or angry may cause them to retreat or play down the situation in an effort to calm you down. It's asking a lot but it's important to curb your emotions. I can say, from experience, that a parent getting overly upset or emotional will cause a child to think twice about coming to you with problems in the future.

It's important that in these conversations you choose your words carefully as your response is critical to recovery from instances of bullying. It's important to make sure that you are not placing the blame on the victim, which often can happen without even realizing it.

Here are some things to avoid saying during these conversations to avoid adding further negative feelings into the situation.

"Why Didn't You Stand Up For Yourself?"

"What Did You Do To Cause This?"

"Toughen Up"

"Get Over It"

Over the course of my high school career these are things that I heard many times from adults and it did more damage than good. It's important to make sure that responsibility for the bully's actions are being place on the bully. If you feel like there may be more to the situation than the victim is letting on, talk to them. Ask them open ended questions but don't let your assumptions or personal feelings about the situation overshadow the issue at hand.

It's also important to remember that bullying is not something someone easily forgets and it can have lasting effects well into adulthood.

Instead, focus on effective listening and let them talk it out without interruption or judgment. Once they have found the courage to speak out and finish what they have to say, the best thing you can do as a parent is offer your support.

When I was in high school and went to my mom with a problem, she would listen to every last word and the very first question she would ask was, "What would you like to do from here?"

This was the best question possible and will be for your child. This places the power back into the hands of the victims and gives them a choice on how to handle the situation at hand. From there, work together to find solutions and support them in each step. Many times you'll find that just being heard and understood is enough to help.

Regardless of the type of bullying taking place it is important to offer not only your help but also get the school involved as well. This is not saying place the full burden of responsibility onto the school but strive to work together to bring a resolution to the bullying. If the school doesn't have a set policy in place for bullying work with them to create one along with a way to report instances.

At the end of the day it's important that everyone work together to make a difference.

Be sure to keep going with these constructive conversations through the incident and beyond. The continued dialogue will create a safe and comfortable environment for your child so they will be more open to coming to you with problems in the future.

Educating the Bullies

When it comes to bullying prevention education, so much emphasis is placed on the victim and ways to battle the bully that very little is done to treat the issue at the root. More often than not, the bully is punished and that is felt to be enough. It's not.

Rather than bullying intervention being limited to simply punishing the bully, steps should be taken to teach them how to interact with others in ways that are more positive.

The first step in this process is teaching the bully to take responsibility for their actions. Regardless of the circumstances, to bully someone is an active choice. Even in situations of peer pressure, a choice was made to proceed. They need to learn that their actions have consequences and that there are real people and lives involved.

It is important to incorporate into the discipline plan social and emotional learning. Asking them to look at the situation of bullying from the perspective of their victim may help them learn empathy and further prevent continued incidents.

Within these lessons work on anger management and impulse control should be prominent lessons as well. Much of the aggression from bullies can be linked to their inability to harness their emotions in stressful situations. Helping them identify triggers for these outburst can assist them in controlling their emotions.

One key step in this "rehabilitation" is working on the bullies issues surrounding their self-esteem. Many times a bully lashes out because they, themselves, feel weak and lacking control. They are so frustrated with these emotions that they take to lashing out on others to feel better about themselves. It's important to work with the bullies on these issues by enhancing their strengths and working to improve on their weaknesses.

From there is making sure that we are teaching them to treat others with respect, to treat them the way that they would want to be treated. Showing them how much power their words and actions can have and, furthermore, showing them the positive influence they can have on others.

What Our Schools Can Do

First and foremost, I feel that when it comes to tacking issues surrounding bullying, it truly takes a village. It is important that parents, students, teachers and administrators all work together to take on this issue.

More and more we are seeing school incorporating anti-bullying policies and practices into schools in accordance with new laws being passed on the state level.

The first step is making sure that the policies being set within the school are clear and realistic. It's great to go above and beyond in creation but if policies can't be enforced then they become useless. From there it's important that these policies are enacted and strictly enforced by teachers and administrators.

Teachers can work to ensure that students have a safe place to talk and always have an adult they can reach out to for help. Much like with parents, when a student comes to you with an issue, practice effective listening. It's also important to pay attention to language. Students won't often come forward and say they are being bullied so the truth may be laying in the subtext of the conversation.

In cases of cyberbullying, it can be important to take action and teach student digital citizenship skills, placing just as much emphasis on this as they would any lesson on interpersonal skills. These skills can help enforce the reality that what happens online not only comes into the offline world but has a very real effects in it. It is important, too, to stress the permanence of the internet and that those hurtful words, pictures and actions can't be taken back.

Continue to encourage students to stand up for one another. Whether online or in the real world, teach them to be the helpful bystanders and make this a continuing lesson. It is important to create a positive school environment and keep it going beyond an awareness week or onetime event.

From there, get the students involved! Work with them to create student-led initiatives where they have control and a voice in creating a positive environment for their peers.

Wrap Up

This is normally the part in the workshop where I would open thing up to question and answer based on the material presented so I'm a little lost right now. Honestly, the amount of time I spent trying to think of what to call this chapter.

When I was in college, I worked as a night manager at a grocery store. In a conversation with the general manager, I expressed my annoyance that we were putting certain policies in place for the store and then lacking in any real follow-up of continuation of the work that had been done.

After a moment of thought, he reminded me of a circus act. You know the one where the performer places a plate on a thin pole and starts it spinning? The act builds as more and more plates are set spinning, but that first one is starting to slow down and topple. Before the performer can move on he has to move back to keep that plate spinning.

This is an example I have found myself bringing up in many moments during workshops and beyond.

It is important that we all work together to get the plate spinning and keep it going.

My hope is that through all of this, some

inspiration and ideas came about for what you can do as a parent, educator, or casual reader to begin to make a different in the lives of young people.

I thank for reading and I truly hope that this was a good first step on the path towards bullying prevention in your community.

About the Author

Josh Gunderson is a graduate of Salem State University in Massachusetts where he earned his BA in both English and Theatre. He is an educational speaker specializing in internet safety and bullying prevention and since 2009 he has spoken at hundreds of schools all over the United States on these topics.

Josh currently resides in Orlando, FL where he can usually be found at a theme park in his free time.

More information about Josh and his education programs can be found on his web site at www.joshgunderson.com

23532663R00031

Printed in Great Britain
by Amazon